LIGHTNING BOLT BOOKS™

W9-CND-716

Let's Visit the Rain Forest

Buffy Silverman

Lerner Publications • Minneapolis

For the Neaton family

Lerner Publications Company
A division of Lerner Publishing Group, Inc.
241 First Avenue North
Minneapolis, MN 55401 USA

For reading levels and more information, look up this title at www.lernerbooks.com.

Library of Congress Cataloging-in-Publication Data

Names: Silverman, Buffy, author.
Title: Let's visit the rain forest / Buffy Silverman.
Other titles: Let us visit the rain forest
Description: Minneapolis : Lerner Publications, [2017] | Series: Lightning bolt books. Biome explorers |
    Audience: Ages 5–8. | Audience: K to grade 3. | Includes bibliographical references and index.
Identifiers: LCCN 2015046090 (print) | LCCN 2015048647 (ebook) | ISBN 9781512411959 (lb : alk.
    paper) | ISBN 9781512412338 (pb : alk. paper) | ISBN 9781512412031 (eb pdf)
Subjects: LCSH: Rain forests—Juvenile literature. | Rain forest ecology—Juvenile literature. | Rain
    forest animals—Juvenile literature.
Classification: LCC QH541.5.R27 S56 2017 (print) | LCC QH541.5.R27 (ebook) | DDC 578.734—dc23

LC record available at http://lccn.loc.gov/2015046090

Manufactured in the United States of America
1-39697-21308-2/24/2016

Table of Contents

A Journey to a Rain Forest

Imagine walking through a rain forest. Monkeys howl from the treetops. Colorful parrots fly overhead.

Howler monkeys can be heard from 3 miles (4.8 kilometers) away!

Leaves block the sunlight. The air feels damp. Water drips from the trees that tower above you.

Tropical rain forests grow in wet places near the equator. There are also temperate rain forests along coastal areas.

This map shows tropical rain forests.

NORTH AMERICA

EUROPE

ASIA

AFRICA

SOUTH AMERICA

AUSTRALIA

Rain forest

ANTARCTICA

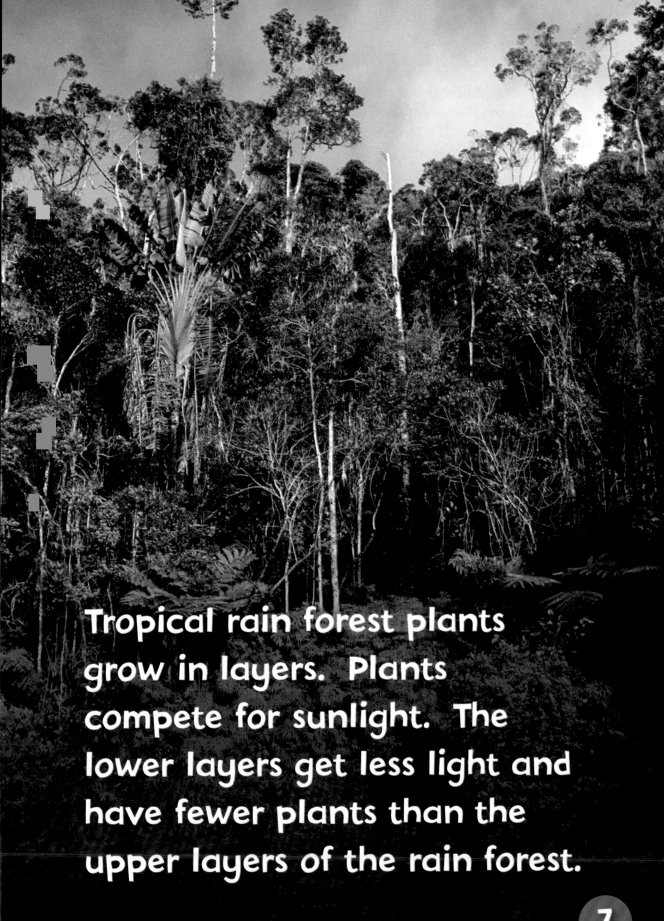

Tropical rain forest plants grow in layers. Plants compete for sunlight. The lower layers get less light and have fewer plants than the upper layers of the rain forest.

The rain forest can get 80 to 400 inches (203 to 1,016 centimeters) of rain each year.

More rain falls in this biome than in any other place on Earth. Even when the rain stops, the water keeps falling through each layer of the rain forest.

But it is not cold in the tropical rain forest. The temperature stays between 70 and 85°F (21 to 29°C) all year.

Temperate rain forests are not as warm as tropical rain forests. They are farther from the equator. Winters are long and wet. Summers are drier.

Temperate rain forests are filled with ocean fog. Water droplets drip down tall trees.

Animals in the Rain Forest

There are more kinds of animals in a rain forest habitat than anywhere else on Earth.

Many rain forest animals live high in the trees. Harpy eagles make huge nests at the top of the forest. They use their strong claws to hunt for food.

Harpy eagles can turn their heads upside down to see their prey.

This sloth hides in a tree.

Sloths hang from branches in the canopy. Green algae in their fur makes them harder to see in the trees.

White bats roost beneath leaves. They bite the leaves into V-shaped tents to keep dry. At night, they fly and find fruit to eat.

Water collects in plants growing in the understory. Poison dart frogs carry their tadpoles from the forest floor to these pools of water. The pools keep the tadpoles safe.

This frog is carrying its tadpoles on its back.

Leaf-cutter ants cut leaves from rain forest plants. The ants carry the leaves to underground nests. Fungus grows on the chewed-up leaves. Then the ants eat the fungus.

Animals in temperate rain forests find food on the ground. Seeds fall from the trees. Birds, chipmunks, and deer gather the seeds.

In the temperate rain forest, most animals live on the ground.

Plants in the Rain Forest

Plants grow everywhere in the warm, wet rain forest. A kapok tree towers over the rest of the rain forest. It can grow 200 feet (61 meters) tall. It has wide roots for support.

Tree branches and leaves in the canopy act like a roof. The waxy leaves repel water. The canopy keeps rain and light from reaching the ground.

Most fruit grows in the canopy of the rain forest.

Orchids have a strong smell to attract birds and insects.

Some plants in the rain forest do not need soil to grow. Flowers such as orchids can grow on the sides of trees.

Small trees and shrubs grow beneath other plants. These plants can grow with little light.

Palms grow in the understory. They have large leaves to catch light and water.

The forest floor is very dark. Only a few plants grow here. Leaves and fruit fall to the ground and decay quickly.

Many trees in the temperate rain forest are one hundred years old.

Giant fir trees grow in temperate rain forests. Mosses hang from their branches. Ferns grow on the ground.

Living in the Rain Forest

Plants and animals depend on one another in the rain forest ecosystem. Trees and other plants grow leaves, fruits, and seeds that animals eat.

Toucans swallow fruit whole. They spread fruit seeds in their droppings.

Butterflies and bats drink nectar from flowers. They carry pollen so flowers can make seeds. Birds eat fruits. New plants grow from seeds in their droppings.

This green snake is called an emerald tree boa.

Animals that hunt need rain forest trees to reach their prey. Snakes climb tall branches. There they find birds, bats, lizards, and monkeys.

Dead plants and animals drop to the forest floor. Insects and mushrooms help these plants and animals decay. Everything works together in the rain forest biome.

People in the Rain Forest

- About fifty million people live in the world's rain forests. The Yanomami people have lived in the rain forest of South America for thousands of years. They use many different plants for food, medicine, and building.

- People around the world depend on rain forests too. We get chocolate, bananas, and other fruits from the rain forest. We also discover new medicines from rain forest plants.

- Rain forest trees make oxygen and help keep the air clean. We must use the rain forest carefully to protect the forest ecosystem.

Biome Extremes

- **Wettest place:** Mawsynram, India (467 inches, or 11,871 millimeters, of rain in a year)

- **Giant leaves:** giant Amazon water lily (8-foot-wide, or 2.5 m, leaves)

- **Tallest trees:** Redwoods in California (379 feet, or 116 m, tall)

- **Oldest rain forest:** Taman Negara, Malaysia (130 million years old)

- **Largest snake:** green anaconda of the Amazon rain forest (more than 550 pounds, or 249 kilograms)

- **Smallest monkey:** pygmy marmoset of the South American rain forests (0.25 pounds, or 0.1 kg—about the weight of a stick of butter)

Glossary

biome: plants and animals in a large area, such as a desert or forest

canopy: the thick layer of leaves and branches that forms the upper part of a forest

ecosystem: an area of connected living and nonliving things

equator: an imaginary east-west line around the middle of Earth. The equator is halfway between the North Pole and South Pole.

habitat: the natural home of plants or animals

nectar: sweet liquid made by a flower to attract insects, bats, and birds

pollen: powder made by a flower that is carried to other flowers to make seeds

repel: to keep something out or away

roost: to rest or sleep

temperate: land that is between the equator and the polar regions

understory: shrubs and trees growing beneath the canopy of a forest

Further Reading

Benoit, Peter. *Tropical Rain Forests.* New York: Children's Press, 2011.

Kids Do Ecology: Rainforest
http://kids.nceas.ucsb.edu/biomes/rainforest.html

National Geographic Kids: 15 Cool Things about Rainforests!
http://www.ngkids.co.uk/science-and-nature/15-cool-things-about-rainforests

Rainforest Alliance: Kids' Corner
http://www.rainforest-alliance.org/kids

Rice, William B. *Amazon Rainforests.* Huntington Beach, CA: Teacher Created Materials, 2012.

Index

Photo Acknowledgments

The images in this book are used with the permission of: © Dirk Ercken/Shutterstock.com, pp. 2, 15; © Jess Kraft/Shutterstock.com, p. 4; © Digital Vision/PhotoDisc/Thinkstock, p. 5; © Laura Westlund/Independent Picture Service, p. 6; © Nigel J. Dennis/Science Source, p. 7; © itman__47/iStock/Thinkstock, p. 8; © tororo reaction/Shutterstock.com, p. 9; © Matt Tilghman/Shutterstock.com, p. 10; © iStockphoto.com/pidjoe, p. 11; © nbiebach/Shutterstock.com, p. 12; © Kjersti Joergensen/Shutterstock.com, p. 13; © LOOK Die Bildagentur der Fotografen GmbH/Alamy, p. 14; © Ryan M. Bolton/Shutterstock.com, p. 16; © iStockphoto.com/oranorth, p. 17; © iStockphoto.com/gionnixxx, p. 18; © AustralianCamera/Shutterstock.com, p. 19; © Chris Fredriksson/Alamy, p. 20; © Morley Read/Alamy, p. 21; © clearviewstock/Shutterstock.com, p. 22; © tusharkoley/Shutterstock.com, p. 23; © pzAxe/Shutterstock.com, p. 24; © Paul S. Wolf/Shutterstock.com, p. 25; © Dennis W. Donohue/Shutterstock.com, p. 26; © Morley Read/Alamy, p. 27; © f9photos/iStock/Thinkstock, p. 31.

Front cover: © Oxford Scientific/Getty Images.

Main body text set in Johann Light 30/36.